THE 20 SECRETS TO A SUCCESSFUL BOOK LAUNCH

KICKSTART

ROBIN WAITE

Bestseling author of **Online Business Startup** and **Take Your Shot**

ROBIN WAITE

First Published in Great Britain 2018

By Robin M. Waite

Copyright © 2018 by Robin M. Waite

All rights reserved. This book or any portion thereof may not be reproduced or used in any manner whatsoever without the express written permission of the publisher except for the use of brief quotations in a book review.

Paperback ISBN 978-0-9957768-3-8

Robin Waite Limited
Stroud House
Russell Street
Stroud
Gloucestershire
GL5 3AN

www.robinwaite.com

PRAISE

"Rob's storytelling and book-launch experience make Kickstart an amazingly quick and easy read, that's packed with dozens of crucial tips for a successful campaign.

Not a single page is wasted, you'll learn something vital every step and find your confidence, towards a more successful launch-day, higher than ever.

This is the most comprehensive book-launch guide I've seen to date."

Harry Barnes, Personal Trainer at Muscle for Life

"A wonderful quick read full of tips and techniques to create your own best seller. Thoroughly recommended."

Ben, Amazon Reader

CONTENTS

	Foreword	1
	Introduction	3
Chapter 1	Proof Copies	5
Chapter 2	Book Landing Page	9
Chapter 3	Email Confirmation	13
Chapter 4	Building Your List	17
Chapter 5	Amazon Upload and Author Page	19
Chapter 6	Kindle Vs Paperback Promotion	23
Chapter 7	MailChimp	25
Chapter 8	SMS Marketing	27
Chapter 9	Audiobook Creation	29
Chapter 10	The Package	33
Chapter 11	'Warm up' Amazon	35
Chapter 12	Launch Day	37
Chapter 13	Follow Up	39
Chapter 14	Ongoing PR	41
Chapter 15	Help a Reporter Out	43
Chapter 16	Amazon Reviews	45
Chapter 17	Goodreads Giveaways and Author Program	47
Chapter 18	Twitter Pinned Post	49
Chapter 19	Amazon Marketplace	51
Chapter 20	Podcast Interviews	53
	How do you Know if This is Working?	55
	About the author	59
	Fearless business	63
	Reading list	65

For Charlotte, Poppy and Sophie

INTRODUCTION

I published my first book, Online Business Startup, with the help of the hybrid publishing team at Rethink Press. It was a real rollercoaster topped off with a thrillingly successful launch into Amazon on Friday 22nd May 2015.

With Online Business Startup it took me eight months to achieve 100 reviews and the best part of 2 years before I got to 200 reviews. The book has remained on the best-seller lists on Amazon for the best part of those two years resulting in thousands of book sales and £1,000s in relatively passive income.

I had one goal in mind when I launched my second book, Take Your Shot, in September 2017; and that was to get 100 reviews within 24 hours, and 200 reviews within six months.

Many people have asked me about my launch campaigns and why they were so successful.

One word.

PLANNING!

I wanted to share my entire launch process with you which I hope will save you time, money and fill in some blanks about the marketing process.

I hope that using my helpful tips you too might be able to achieve a number one bestselling book and experience the pride of having the inimitable words '#1 Bestseller' appear next to your name and book listing.

I'll take you right the way through to achieving that number one ranking and see your business transformed by the power of a successful book launch.

If you'd told me this time last year that I'd be writing my second, let alone my third book, I'd have laughed in your face. But after the success of Online Business Startup and Take Your Shot, I wanted to write this book for two reasons.

Firstly, I thoroughly enjoy the writing and book marketing processes, and I wanted to share that experience through the medium of another book.

I've spoken to many people since launching Online Business Startup, and many of those people intimated that it was such an amazing achievement, writing a book and becoming an Amazon Bestseller. I found this strange because I didn't feel as though it was that great an achievement, primarily because I found it to be an easy and enjoyable process.

It's about perception, and perhaps if you haven't written a book, it may seem like quite an undertaking. Equally, some people will find writing easy; others will find it hard.

But, writing a book is just half the battle.

People then need to be able to find your book to buy it.

If you've already started writing the book, are planning the launch or want to give it a Kickstart, then this book is for you.

The most common comments I received were, 'I don't know where to start,' 'I don't have the time,' 'I don't have enough knowledge,' 'I'm not sure who'll buy my book.' I believe that if you put the principles in this book into practice, you'll find it easier than you imagined to successfully launch your book into Bestsellter status.

I will explain the techniques I used to launch and promote my book which will form part of the campaign you will use in taking your book to market.

Producing a book is one thing, but if you want the book to reach a wider audience, you need to have a book launch and undertake marketing and PR activities. Getting to the top of the Amazon bestseller lists is quite a feat; maintaining that bestseller ranking is a whole other ball game.

Kickstart is structured as a 'How to Guide'; this is because a book launch is a mechanical process. There are specific instructions to follow via a delineated timeline which I have created.

My writing style is quite personal; I will explain how I went about launching Online Business Startup and Take Your Shot on Amazon. I don't hold back with my content as I want to give as much information as I possibly can.

I'm assuming you've already written, or are in the process of writing, your book. Therefore, my goal in writing Kickstart is to help at least one person launch a book successfully, attain the #1 Bestseller ranking, and maintain it.

If you break the book launch process down into some smaller tasks, it will be more manageable.

I hope that this book sparks your imagination and gets you started on the thoroughly enjoyable activity of launching your book.

HOW TO USE THIS BOOK:

Using Kickstart is simple.

The book is laid out as a time-line starting from 60 days leading up to your book launch, and onto the marketing activities you must do after your launch to ensure you achieve and most important KEEP your Bestseller spot.

If you have any questions please go to my website and to find out more about my Fearless Business Coaching programme:

<u>http://robinwaite.com/fearless/application</u>

CHAPTER 1
LAUNCH MINUS 60 DAYS: PROOF COPIES

Now that you've written your book, and had it designed and typewritten, the first thing you will likely want next is to hold a physical copy of your book.

The common mistake most people make at this point is to attempt to dump their book onto Kindle Direct Publishing, CreateSpace and Lightning Source. All require a certain amount of technical knowledge. And my recommendation would be to let a professional take care of this to avoid any unnecessary tantrums.

However, if you're desperate for proof copies, either ask your publisher or use a service like DoxZoo to have a short print run printed.

DoxZoo is more expensive that Lightning Source and CreateSpace by about 25%. The quality is much better. The paper is thicker and whiter than the two mainstream print-on-demand printing houses.

Either way, ensure you order at least 100 copies of your book; because you're going to give them away.

Give them away?

Yes, give them away. From a business perspective, this may sound counter-intuitive. However there are a lot of books out there as well as busy business people, so you need a strong incentive to get everyone to buy into your book launch.

The second biggest mistake I see new authors make is to launch their campaign with no 'tribe' behind them supporting their launch.

The reason for this is because everyone leads incredibly busy lives these days and the likelihood of even some of your most avid fans being online on your launch day is slim. So, you are going to offer free copies of your book to incentivise them to buy the Kindle on the day and leave a review.

When I handed out the first copies of Take Your Shot at a networking event a number of the guests told me how special it made them feel to hold one of the first copies. They volunteered to help with the launch there and then and posted photos of the book all over Social Media after the event.

Subsequently, this led to some people requesting further copies, adding fuel the campaign right from the word go.

The key thing here though is the 'Exchange'.

"I will be gifting you a pre-release/review copy of Take Your Shot in exchange for your help on the launch day. Is that ok?" – Almost everyone said, "Yes! I'd love to help!"

It's important to tell your subjects when your expected launch date is and what is expected of them.

Finally, collect their contact details. I'll be talking more about how to do this in the next couple of chapters.

KICKSTART

CHAPTER 2
LAUNCH MINUS 54 DAYS: BOOK LANDING PAGE

OPTION 1: THE LONG WAY

I am at a slight advantage with Step 2 from having worked in the web design industry for ten years+.

The book landing page is central to your launch campaign. It provides you and your book with identity online and a place to direct readers to register their interest in taking part in your launch promotion.

Don't underestimate the time required to get this page set up and tested thoroughly. Your landing page can be in build while you are waiting for your book to list on Amazon. If a web designer is going to build a landing page for you, then ensure that they have plenty of notice and the capacity to build it for you in time for your launch.

The landing page needs to be nothing more than a 3-page website which uses the same branding and artwork as your book cover. It only needs a few basic details on it:

Home Page – Use the content from your book's back cover with your book's title, strapline and main bullet points. Get a 3D version of your book cover designed, they look great online. Create a call-to-action button which leads your user to your Book Launch page. Also, include an About the Author page with your professional headshot – it adds personality to the page. Add some testimonials, and the home page is complete.

Book Launch Page – Include the following:

- When the launch date is
- A clear statement saying 'Don't buy the book YET!'
- MailChimp Sign-up Form (see Step 3)
- A list of Gifts and Bonuses – this is typically a review copy of the book which MUST be FREE (if it is not free you are in breach of Amazon's terms and conditions, you cannot pay people to buy or review your book).
- An explanation as to why you are doing a book launch
- Outline the steps the reader is required to complete the launch sequence

A N Other Page – I wanted to put in an extra page about what the reader could expect to find in my book, so I created a 'Core Values' page which included a breakdown of the three main topics covered in the book. You might choose to add something different, such as a sample chapter or endorsements.

You may choose to add a blog to the landing site to that you can add updates about your book launch and build a campaign.

Once the launch is complete, you have a platform to carry on adding content against to generate leads for your book once the launch is over.

As an alternative to creating a traditional website-based landing page you could try out LeadPages - leadpages.net/ or ClickFunnels - clickfunnels.com/ which are custom lead-generation and landing-page tools. Leadpages and ClickFunnels are optimised for building lists but require some technical understanding about building funnels.

One major benefit of having a custom book website built is that you will have a legacy site which can remain in place once the promotion ends.

You could, of course, use both options (landing page website and lead generation tools) if you want to get maximum impact.

To view my landing page and get a feel for the design and layout, please take a look at onlinebusinessstartup.co.uk

OPTION 2: THE SHORT WAY

Since launching both books, I've discovered some other fantastic tools.

The best data-capture form building thingie I've found recently is called TypeForm. It's easy to customise and embed on your website (if you are already using something like WordPress for example). But the beauty of TypeForm is that you don't need to embed it. You can customise it to your branding and then direct prospects to the custom URL that TypeForm provide.

There's no complicated website, or technical hurdles to overcome.

The free version of TypeForm allows up to ten questions, which is plenty for this exercise as the only real information to get:

- Name
- Email Address
- Mobile Number
- Address
- Option to request PDF or Paperback

Once you've collected the data using TypeForm you can then use a 'micro-tasking' tool such as Zapier or If This Then That (IFTTT) to add the TypeForm date into MailChimp or ActiveCampaign as these email automation tools will handle the new General Data Processing Regulations which come into force in May 2018.

I talk about why Email Confirmation is important in the next chapter.

CHAPTER 3
LAUNCH MINUS 45 DAYS: EMAIL CONFIRMATION

First of all, you need to know why it's important to collect data during your launch campaign.

Data capture is vital as most human beings seem to be forgetful, lazy or too damned busy to remember to get involved in our stuff. Therefore you collect their name, email address and mobile telephone number so that, with their permission of course, you can send them reminders before, during and after your book launch.

OPTION 1: MAILCHIMP SIGN-UP

I used MailChimp; you can, of course, use any of the Cloud-based automated email tools available. I find MailChimp to be the easiest and most reliable to use.

You will need to register for a MailChimp account and create a 'list'. In the list, you can then create forms. I used the 'naked' form which I could then embed on my page and style up to match the rest of the landing page which I had built in Step 2.

Collect as little information as possible to make it easier for your supporters to complete. first name,surname, email address, and mobile number should suffice.

You can create 'template' emails within MailChimp. I suggest you create a banner image which is 600 pixels wide. The height doesn't matter too much but try and keep it to 100 pixels if you can to ensure the contents of your emails don't fall below the bottom of the viewing pane.

This banner is a JPEG image which is designed for one specific purpose: to appear at the top of your MailChimp emails. It will be used on all of your outbound emails from MailChimp and should contain your logo at the very least. The banner ensures that any emails MailChimp sends on your behalf are all consistently branded and recognisable by the recipient.

Test the emails thoroughly yourself before sending them to your list. When a new subscriber signs up to your promotion or free chapter download they will receive a confirmation from MailChimp. The confirmation is something called a 'double opt-in' and is MailChimp's way of ensuring that the people who sign up to your list want to receive emails from you and that their email addresses exist.

During testing ensure that the confirmation email comes through. There's nothing worse than launching a sign-up form only to find it doesn't work. People interested in taking part in your promotion will only come to your website or landing page once to complete the form. So double and triple check it.

OPTION 2: AUTORESPONSE FROM TYPEFORM

TypeForm has several other great features. The one which you will use is the Autoresponse feature. An autoresponse is the email TypeForm sends to those completing your form to acknowledge receipt of their details.

You can customise it with a message outlining when the launch date is planned, with full instructions on what's expected of them on launch day.

At this point, you must start sharing your goals for the campaign with those who are volunteering to help so that they buy into your purpose. I was very clear during my launch for Take Your Shot that I wanted to achieve 100 reviews on launch day. The #1 Bestseller spot was almost superfluous for launch as I know that 100 reviews would ensure my book would be consistently competitive in its respective categories.

KICKSTART

CHAPTER 4
LAUNCH MINUS 45 DAYS: BUILDING YOUR LIST

Once the landing page is set up detailing the gifts and bonuses for taking part in your book launch and your sign-up form is embedded and styled up, you are now ready to start filling the list up.

The primary objective of building your book launch list is to get a feel for how many registrations of interest you have in advance of your chosen launch date. The numbers will depend very much on which categories Amazon has chosen for you but here is a breakdown of how I felt I needed my campaign to go to gain a #1 Bestseller ranking on Amazon and to break into the top 1,000 Amazon Sales Rank.

My magic number was 40. All I was aiming to sell on launch day was 40 copies of my book, and I didn't care about whether they bought the Kindle or paperback. As it turns out, typically about 60% of people buy the Kindle, and 40% buy the paperback (based on the verified purchases shown in the review section of my book).

Total Number of Contacts Including friends, family, acquaintances, work colleagues, anyone who I knew in some way.	750
Registrations of Interest These were defined as pledges on Facebook, Twitter, by word of mouth or in passing that the person would support me on the day.	150
Actual Sign-ups These were registrations of interest who then actually went on to add themselves to my mailing list via the sign-up form on the landing page (and successfully confirm their email address).	80
Purchases Somewhat speculative; however, I knew from my list of sign-ups that some people who would 'definitely' buy the book on the day. And others who were somewhat 'flaky' or were likely to be busy on the day; and therefore wouldn't buy the book or review it. I estimated that about half of my list would buy the book.	35-40

I felt confident from pre-marketing and promotions which Amazon had run on my book that 40 sales would be plenty to achieve at least one #1 bestseller rank in a category which Amazon had chosen for my book.

CHAPTER 5
LAUNCH MINUS 21 DAYS: AMAZON UPLOAD AND AUTHOR PAGE

The process of getting everything organised on Amazon can be slow. It is essential to hold off on your book launch until Amazon has correctly indexed your book for both the Kindle and paperback versions.

THE NEXT SECTION BELOW IS FOR THOSE OF YOU WHO ARE PLANNING ON SELF-PUBLISHING.

For the Kindle, you will need to create an account with Kindle Direct Publishing: kdp.amazon.com/

Once registered and logged in you will be presented with a wizard which will guide you through the process of creating your first book title.

KINDLE AND PAPERBACK CATEGORIES ON KDP AND CREATESPACE

Pay close attention to this section. It is vital you research your Amazon categories thoroughly.

There are several thousand book categories available to choose from on Amazon. Many are incredibly competitive, but there are some categories which are not competitive in the slightest.

I have two key reminders for you when choosing your categories.

Amazon categories are nested, i.e. Books > Small Business & Finance > Small Business and Entrepreneurship.

The biggest mistake many self-published authors make is choosing a top-level category for their book to be placed in. These have more books in them and are therefore more competitive.

TOP TIP: Choose a category which is nested 4 or 5 levels down in the category hierarchy.

If your book does well in a lower category, it will start rising the rankings in its respective parent category.

Secondly, there is a temptation to choose irrelevant categories which have fewer books in them and so are naturally less competitive. However, it will look odd if your book appears in Crocheting and Knitting if it is a Business and Finance book.

You get to choose one or two categories for your book when

you upload it; Amazon does the rest using its hyper-intelligent algorithm.

Although Online Business Startup ended up placed in the Trading and Investing category. Great because it was #1 but many of the books in the same category were about Bitcoin and other financial trading related stuff which Online Business Startup definitely wasn't about.

Once you have created your book title, it will appear on the Bookshelf. Kindle versions go live quickly, the KDP site says within approximately 72 hours it will be available to purchase online. The KDP website has an amazing help section which guides you through the many aspects of the KDP program; this is available at the following URL: kdp.amazon.com/help

If you intend to create a paperback or hardback edition of your book, you will need to register with CreateSpace: createspace.com/

CreateSpace is the publishing platform owned by Amazon and is a platform to distribute books through internet retail outlets (including Amazon), your website, bookstores, retailers, libraries and academic institutions. You can order professional services through CreateSpace such as cover design, copy-editing and preparing your documents so that they meet CreateSpace's submission requirements.

Once you or your publisher have uploaded your book, the paperback will appear on Amazon several days after the Kindle edition.

However.

DO NOT LAUNCH YET!

If your paperback is delivered via print-on-demand, then there are a couple of quirks that you need to look out for. When your book is first listed it is marked as 'Out of Stock'; after about two weeks the delivery period changes to '1-2 Months'.

Do not launch during this period because if potential buyers go to buy the paperback and see either message, this will likely put them off buying.

Wait until the paperback shows as available and 'In Stock'. Your launch can happen at any time once this has happened but you want to remove as many barriers to people buying your book as possible on the launch day.

The Author Page is something you will need to set up, but this isn't possible until your book is added to KDP successfully. When your Kindle and paperback versions are displaying on Amazon then go ahead and set up your Author Page.

Amazon's Author Central is available at the following website address:

authorcentral.amazon.co.uk/

Ensure that you upload professional photographs, link up your Twitter account and add your author biography. Then type your name into Amazon's search box, it's quite satisfying to see yourself on your author page.

CHAPTER 6
PAPERBACK VERSUS KINDLE PROMOTION

I have seen a lot of authors focus on promoting either the paperback or the Kindle, rarely both.

Typical Kindle offers include a 99p Kindle promotion on the launch day so that it is cheaper and more accessible for those taking part in the launch campaign.

You could offer a FREE Kindle deal on launch as well. Making the Kindle free for a few days removes all barriers to readers accessing and reading your book. However, the free downloads don't count towards your paid Kindle ranking.

What happens during a free Kindle deal is that your book will appear in the Free Kindle Charts on Amazon for a period. When your book reverts to being paid the residual traffic from releasing your book for free will result in some sales.

What's more interesting is focussing on Paperback sales during a launch campaign.

Kindle is very accessible, and as a result, there are approximately ten times the numbers of Kindle books available as there are paperbacks.

What this means is less competition in the paperback category rankings on Amazon. Less competition means you need fewer sales of your paperback to occupy the higher rankings in the various Amazon categories.

The Paperback version of Online Business Startup was at #1 in its respective categories a long time before the Kindle was.

I'd be tempted to focus on a 99p Paperback campaign next time over a 99p Kindle campaign.

CHAPTER 7
LAUNCH MINUS 14 DAYS: MAILCHIMP

There are three emails which you need to set up in MailChimp to help automate the process of promoting your book launch. The stats in the brackets represents the successful open rate of the campaign to warm prospects:

1. **Welcome** – A simple welcome email which thanks to the recipient for signing up and explains the process of the launch, what they need to do and when (59.7% open rate).
2. **Launch Day** – A scheduled email to go out between 8 am, and 9 am on the day of the book launch. This email contains a link to the Amazon book page; a big thank you message and instructions on what to do after they buy your book, i.e. An invitation to purchasers to read and review your book within two weeks of the launch date (67.6% open rate).
3. **Follow Up** – A final scheduled email to go out four days after launch to remind people taking part in the promotion to leave reviews (63.2% open rate).

I found the stats on open rates quite remarkable – much lower than I had anticipated. The low open rate is an important reason for oversubscribing your list in the run-up to launch. The main reasons that the open rates were lower than I had anticipated were for the following reasons:

- Failure to read instructions properly
- The sign-up and double opt-in failed, so they never received the email
- Their email application spammed or junked the email so, again, it never arrived. Google even placed my emails into a special 'promotions' folder in Gmail email accounts.
- The email didn't display as expected in certain email applications. Therefore the recipient didn't see any of the calls-to-action in the email.
- General technical incompetence!

In this day and age, technology is supposed to help us, but on launch day be prepared to call and speak to as many of those who have pledged to help as possible. You will be helping them to overcome these minor technical hurdles to complete the task and 'manually' achieve higher success rates. I even spent some time with one person tutoring them on how to purchase a product on Amazon.

CHAPTER 8
LAUNCH MINUS DAYS: SMS MARKETING

With Online Business Startup I achieved fantastic open rates and click-through rates with email. In the last two years, however, the landscape has shifted dramatically with email marketing and even to warm lists I was only achieving 40-60% open rates and 5% click-through rates at best.

As with everything, I thought to myself, "There has to be a better way!" At that point, a text message pinged through on my phone. It was spam, I used to go to Cheltenham Races regularly, and this was a message from a tipster I'd subscribed to a long while ago.

Naturally, the text message pissed me off, but it was purely because I was no longer interested. It was at this point I thought to myself, "If I can promote my books using SMS without annoying people this could work well."

And it did.

I used SMS to promote Take Your Shot the open rates were astonishing 99%, albeit unsurprisingly. The surprising bit though was the click-through rate. Over 60%.

I'd carried out some research and found a superb tool called TextMagic. TextMagic sends out SMS messages to groups of contacts that you can add into it as though they are coming from your mobile phone.

Best of all, I had contacts messaging me back almost immediately saying they had bought the book and reviewed it. Real-time feedback.

I would suggest this was the single-most effective step in achieving 100 reviews within 24 hours.

The secret sauce I discovered, though, was not to abuse this new found power. I recognised that any more than two or three messages to individuals would annoy them.

So, I kept my SMS campaign to its barest minimum sending only three messages:

1. 48 hours before launch day reminding them about the imminent book launch.
2. On the morning of the launch with a link to purchase the book.
3. Seven days post-launch with a link which would take them straight to the book review section on Amazon.

And that was it.

Click-through rates went up throughout the campaign across the three messages as people got more engaged.

It contributed hugely to the success of the campaign.

CHAPTER 9
LAUNCH MINUS 8 DAYS: AUDIOBOOK CREATION

I didn't eventually get around to investigating publishing an Audiobook version of Online Business Startup until approximately eight months after it launched. And, boy, did I wish I had launched the audiobook earlier; especially when I realised how easy it was to get a book published in audiobook format.

So, why publish in Audiobook format?

Well, my book has sold well in Kindle and Paperback versions, but the audiobook has consistently outsold both of these combined since launch by a factor of 3-1.

Income wise it is difficult to say whether the audiobook is more profitable than the other formats. However, it was such a quick win for me given the hard work is found in writing the book in the first place.

So, the moment the Kindle or Paperback version of your book goes live on Amazon you are ready to start the process of building your audiobook.

I used another Amazon service called ACX.com which made the process straightforward. You can upload your book as a "project" and then start taking auditions from narrators using a sample chapter from your book. Once you have listened to all of the auditions and chosen your favourite, you can then book them to narrate and edit your audiobook.

There are three options:

1. You **pay per hour** of recorded audio. This ranges from $100/hr up to $600+/hr.
2. You can agree a **50/50 revenue share** with the narrator.
3. Get a good quality microphone and **do it yourself**.

Given that Amazon and ACX take 60% of the revenue anyway, I felt doing a 50/50 revenue split was a quick win as for me it was about getting the initial audiobook out in a lean format to as wide an audience as possible.

I've since discovered it's within the narrator's interests to market the book on your behalf because they earn more from that arrangement. If you pay-per-hour, then you get to keep all of the 40% of the royalties left over but have to pay the up-front costs.

Once they have recorded and uploaded each of the chapters, it is then your responsibility to proof-listen to the entire audiobook and recommends edits. Once approved the audiobook will be available on Amazon and Audible in approx. 7-10 days.

Do this immediately! It's such a quick and easy win!

BONUS: In reading the book out loud you will find plenty of mistakes in your book. It is the best means of testing the content of your book. I narrated Take Your Shot myself and stumbled across about 40 mistakes in the book that my proofreaders missed.

The list is critical. You, as the author, need to leverage your list of contacts to make your Amazon book launch a success. However, perhaps you know someone else who is a Key Person of Influence and sitting on a large list of contacts. Perhaps you can create a joint venture with that person and ask them to promote your book launch. BUT the key thing is to build sign-ups within your marketing list. That is the only way you can GUARANTEE your emails will hit the number of people you had planned and need on launch day. Aim BIG!

CHAPTER 10
LAUNCH MINUS 5 DAYS: THE PACKAGE

"Oh look! My box of books has arrived"

This is the element of your launch campaign which is going to be staged. I wanted a positive message to send out a few days before my book launch to re-capture my supporters' attention.

I had ordered 50 copies of Online Business Startup to be delivered to my office for post-launch PR purposes. These arrived a month or so before the book launch so had been lying around in their box for a while.

I organised for my photographer to come in and take some professional shots of me opening up the box and posing happily with my box of books.

Five days before launch I posted a reminder message on several Facebook groups and on my timeline alongside these new photographs. It created a fantastic buzz, looked professional and encouraged a further 18 sign-ups to my launch campaign in the first hour. My busiest list-building day by far.

Perhaps you can think of other similar activities like this in the build-up to your book launch.

CHAPTER 11
LAUNCH MINUS 3 DAYS: 'WARM UP' AMAZON

I knew that starting from zero mph on Amazon would make the task of achieving a good ranking on Amazon even more challenging. I wanted to engineer a rolling start to give me some momentum on launch day. I did this by encouraging some of my closest work colleagues to buy the book at strategic times in the run-up to launch day.

Three copies on launch minus three days, three further purchases on launch minus two days, and finally four purchases were made on the final day before launch. As a result, my Amazon rank jumped from #100,000 up to #30,000 on the evening before the launch.

I would say this was the second cornerstone of my successful launch, with success here defined as getting a #1 rank in one or more categories on Amazon (Kindle or paperback). If I hadn't warmed up Amazon in this way, I feel I would not have achieved anywhere near the success that I did.

I sent out review copies of the book to strategic people ahead of the launch campaign to build reviews on or before launch day. This meant that when those who had pledged to buy the book went to the book page on Amazon, it had already attained some credibility and positive reviews, which would hopefully encourage others to buy the book on the day.

CHAPTER 12
LAUNCH DAY

Hit refresh lots.

Deplete your entire smartphone battery.

On the launch day, I was on a train somewhere between home and London without a mobile phone signal when my scheduled email went out reminding everyone to go and buy their copy of the book. As soon as I passed through Swindon and 4G returned I was frantically hitting refresh on my mobile phone to see how the book sales were progressing. The good news was that the ranking had improved slightly.

However, during my 10 am meeting, the rankings went down!

DISASTER!

My heart sank, I felt completely deflated having put all this effort into the launch only to see it fail at the last minute.

By 1 pm, when the meeting finished, it was on the way BACK UP again. I only had about 30% battery left on my phone at this point and an agonising tube ride during which I couldn't get online again.

By 2 pm, midway through my second meeting, the ranks

had rocketed: #1 in multiple categories across paperback and Kindle.

It ended up exceeding my expectations by a factor of ten, plus some. I went to the nearest pub and had a celebratory beer. What a feeling!!

A special mention and thank you to Gary Ward, author of *What the Foot?* And Founder of Anatomy in Motion for his patience during that meeting, and for joining in with my excitement when *Online Business Startup* reached #1.

CHAPTER 13
LAUNCH PLUS 3 DAYS: FOLLOW UP

Seriously, follow up!

Following on from a successful launch, you now have to start contacting people and asking them to leave reviews for your book.

Nagging people, at the time, was out of character for me because I was now basically begging anyone who hadn't bought the book to go and buy it and anyone who had bought the book but hadn't yet reviewed it to go and review it.

I was amazed at how many people had sworn on their mother's life that they would buy a copy of my book only to find out they had forgotten or were busy on the day.

So, follow up, beg, do someone a favour, do whatever it takes to get that extra purchase or review.

Most of all do anything you can to keep on getting people to buy it. Nagging people for reviews is ultimately what will help your book to remain visible at the top of Amazon for the longest possible time.

CHAPTER 14
LAUNCH PLUS 7 DAYS: ONGOING PR

Over the following few days, the #1 Bestseller rank remained in place, and it was a good 5-6 days before it started to fade down the rankings. The good news is that as time goes on it is still holding its own in several prestigious categories.

While Online Business Startup's not always holding that #1 spot, it does quite often pop back up to Bestseller status every now and again when there is an influx of sales.

The hard work is essentially done, and I have now achieved fantastic reviews from some wonderful people for both Online Business Startup and Take Your Shot.

I cannot describe how humbled I was by all the support shown throughout both of my book launches.

The work does not stop here though!

I am now working the PR machine. Immediately after the

launch, the local press approached me to write an article about the book coming out, which appeared shortly after the launch.

On an ongoing basis, I continue to work on PR for the book to increase its reach and coverage. I typically send out copies of the book to magazine editors and journalists whose readership I feel it might be appropriate for, as well as to as many influential people I know and meet throughout my travels at networking events and speaking gigs.

CHAPTER 15
HELP A REPORTER OUT

There is a great website called HARO – helpareporter.com – which matches up reporters, journalists and bloggers with experts.

If you answer a question posted by a reporter, they will mention you in the article they are writing, so it's a good opportunity to promote your book.

I have had some successes with submitting tips and stories via HARO mostly increased traffic to my website and social media channels.

My one tip would be to make sure that once you have registered with HARO, select which categories of queries you want to receive.

Otherwise, the emails become a bit long and laborious to go through. I've just filtered the questions I receive down to Business and UK.

I give away free copies of the book to potential customers and encourage people I meet to buy a copy of either book and leave their review. Doing this helps to raise the book's (and my own) profile.

KICKSTART

CHAPTER 16
AMAZON REVIEWS

Typically you have to gift the book to the reviewer in question, but it is a small price to pay if they leave a positive review of your book on Amazon. Reviews are what will encourage others to buy it.

Reviewers must state in their review that they were gifted a copy of the book in exchange for an impartial review.

I have electronic (.mobi and PDF) versions of my book available to gift to people in return for reviews which they can read on their Kindle devices, and also a stock of paperback copies which I can send out at a moment's notice.

Don't forget reviewers are reviewing your book on a voluntary basis, so the correct etiquette is 1) not to pester them and 2) make it as easy as possible for them to access your book.

Finally, DO FOLLOW UP. Leave it a reasonable enough time for your reviewers to have read your book before sending a brief follow-up email reminding them to offer a review; 4 weeks is probably plenty of time. I tend to only send one follow-up email because if they haven't reviewed it in 4 weeks, it is unlikely they ever will.

Reviews have played a major part in sustaining the books' sales since the launch, and I see them now as being the most important factor in keeping the books alive on Amazon.

With Online Business Startup, I set a target of achieving 50 positive reviews within two months of launch. This target was quite specific because it was intended to place my book up there with those currently doing well in my Amazon categories. During the next 6-12 months, I achieved 100+ reviews, which gave the book another boost in its categories and ensured it appeared within the top 2-3 books in its chosen categories on a regular basis.

Having realised the value of reviews for Online Business Startup, it made sense for reviews to be central to the marketing campaign for Take Your Shot.

The target for 100 reviews in 24 hours was set.

CHAPTER 17
GOODREADS GIVEAWAYS & AUTHOR PROGRAM

Goodreads is the largest website in the world for book readers to make recommendations and share books they love with their friends - goodreads.com/

Within Goodreads, you can add your library of books directly from Amazon, as well as track the ones you might want to read and add them to your bookshelf. There are Book Lists created by other users on Goodreads which are tagged by various keywords and genres. You can view Goodreads lists here - goodreads.com/list and browse Goodreads lists by tag using the following URL: goodreads.com/list/tag/

I try and go to Goodreads regularly and add books to the various book lists created by others. Yes, I do add my own to those lists, but I also make recommendations for other books that I feel will also add value to a list. I only add my book to relevant lists; there is no point in trying to game or deceive the system.

Do not add your book to all of the lists all in one go. Gradually add your book to one or two lists per day so that you get a gradual increase in the presence of your book on Goodreads.

Finally, Goodreads has an Author Program which allows you to 'own' books which you have authored. You have to apply for the Author Program and, if you are accepted, Goodreads will link up your existing Goodreads account with your author account.

- At which point you can:
- Add pictures and a biography
- Write blog articles
- Add events such as book signings and speaking gigs
- Share excerpts from your book
- Post videos
- Promote your book via giveaways, advertise in the community and start discussions on your profile

You can see more information about the Goodreads Author Program here: goodreads.com/author/program

CHAPTER 18
TWITTER PINNED POST

A quick and simple tip: write a popular tweet about your book alongside a pic of the book cover and a link to your book page on Amazon and then pin it to the top of your Twitter page.

Having a pinned post referencing your book means that whenever someone looks you up one of the first things they see is a tweet about your book.

You could use a social media scheduling tool such as Buffer or Meet Edgar and post multiple regular 'promotional' tweets about your book in amongst your usual tweets. Extra social media posts will drive traffic to your book page.

CHAPTER 19
AMAZON MARKETPLACE

If you are producing print-on-demand books via Lightning Source, Create Space or DoxZoo another means of getting wider coverage is to add your book to the 'Amazon Marketplace' listings.

Ok, so the beauty of print-on-demand is that Amazon fulfils your order for you. However, through the Amazon Marketplace, I can undercut the price at which Amazon fulfils my book orders while making the same amount of profit.

It means that I have to keep stock of my book, print the shipping label, pack a book into an envelope and walk a hundred metres up to the Post Office. However, it also means that my book appears as a standard listing and a discounted listing within the Marketplace.

Most of all I see who is buying my book through the Marketplace as I am in control of printing the shipping labels.

When I ship my books, I can send a personalised note,

invitation to an event or gift if I choose, or just encouragement to leave a review.

Although, I'll be honest, it's a faff to have to print labels, pack the books and march off down to the Post Office each day.

CHAPTER 20
PODCAST INTERVIEWS

This section isn't just about Podcast interviews, by the way, just to make sure that's clear.

The purpose of this chapter is to illustrate that the power of leveraging another person's audience is where the secret sauce of marketing lies.

Podcast hosts like to have guests on their shows.

These guests are normally influential people in their own rights.

Podcast guests are more palatable if they have written a book which they then send out to podcast hosts to read.

Podcasts have subscribers; normally lots of them.

Therefore it makes sense for authors to market their books via Podcasts. The hosts will give their guests the opportunity to mention their book(s) and any offers at the end of the interview.

Another benefit of podcasts is that the audience you are positioned in front of will typically be your ideal target market as well.

There are currently over 420,000 podcasts to choose from.

I've heard rumours of one hardly-known author who guested on 200 podcasts in a single year. As a result, the income from his books runs into $10,000s every month.

Podcasts are 'evergreen' so if you can guest on the right podcasts then the marketing potential runs on and on, making you money and raising your profile while you sleep.

HOW DO YOU KNOW IF THIS IS WORKING?

That's all great news Rob, but how do I know whether this is working or not?

The first one is easy; you'll see an increase in your book sales as time goes on. You can measure this by running reports in your KDP, CreateSpace and Lightning Source control panels.

Secondly, revenue from book sales will increase. There is a 90-day delay in getting credited for Paperback sales, so it takes a while for these to start arriving in your bank account.

I set up separate lines in my accounting package for my books so that I can track sales revenue month-to-month.

Your book will begin to rise through the rankings on Amazon. Don't be fooled though; a higher rank doesn't automatically lead to more sales. Amazon's ranking algorithm is based on numerous factors, not just sales alone.

Finally, your rankings across multiple categories on Amazon will begin to 'close together'.

What I mean by this is that when your book first ranks on Amazon, it might be #8 in Category A and #167 in Category

B. As your launch and marketing campaign gathers pace the categories will begin to close together. If in Category A your book is at #8, and your campaign is successful, its rank in Category B might close into #16.

Eventually, when your book appears at #1, #2 or #3 in one Category A, it will appear in the top 3 in Category B as well.

NEXT STEPS

Did you launch your book?

Was it successful?

If so, then I would love to hear from you.

Please email me, robin@robinwaite.com.

All feedback, comments, tips or amendments which you would like to suggest for future editions of Kickstart would also be welcomed.

As I mentioned at the start, I have simply written about how I went about launching my books. That doesn't necessarily mean it's the right way to do it. You may have some great tips which will help others to launch their books.

MY OFFER TO YOU!

Finally, if you are willing to leave me a 'Verified Purchase' review on Amazon for **Kickstart**, then I would be happy to offer a 30-minute call about your next product or book launch by way of a thank you.

Using the same email address as above please send me a screen-grab of your review on the Amazon page, and we'll get a date booked into the diary.

ABOUT THE AUTHOR

The first job I took was a paper round, the longest one in the village I lived in, and it paid the most amount of money. The tips I collected every Christmas for four years were bigger than any of the other delivery boys and girls. It meant I could afford to buy two or three CDs a week whereas most of my peers struggled to afford one or two per month.

Soon I was investing my paper-round money in second-hand CDs and selling them at my school to my peers so that I could afford the latest albums and the best Sony hi-fi I could afford.

Not knowing what business I wanted to start; at 18 I worked as a systems analyst, which gave me an enormous insight into systems and processes but my methods resulted in staff in the company I worked at being made redundant. The money wasn't great, so by 22, I'd started a great sideline selling grade-B laptops. I made enough money to quit my job and, in one summer, made over £40,000. Mostly cash (declared, I might add) but that money was sat on the end of my bed. I did what any savvy 22-year-old would have done and bought a car, and booked a holiday with my girlfriend to Florida to see her brother.

While out in Florida I got a call from an old colleague to start up a creative agency.

My design agency wasn't like any other; ordinarily, a new client would submit a request-for-quote, which would trigger this game of "design agency ping-pong." This involved months of back and forth between the agency and customer. I knew there had to be a better way than doing everything remotely; so I created a series of intensive 1-to-1 workshops.

The workshops involved the client working directly with a strategy expert and either a developer or designer – depending on whether it was a website or branding workshop. Typically, this would take 1-2 days.

Logo design, for example; is a process which can take up to eight weeks to create a professional logo. This lengthy process is down to poor communication or lack of time. We charged £60 per hour, and a logo might generate 8-10 hours of chargeable work during that eight-week game of design agency ping-pong.

I invited the client in for a one-to-one, 1-day branding workshop. The process had seven steps with clearly defined outcomes. We charged a fixed price which was £1,495, nearly three times the hourly rate previously charged. I offered a 100% money back guarantee. I did the same with websites and created a 2-day prototyping workshop. It started to slot into place.

Four years later.

ABOUT THE AUTHOR

After speeding down Frocester Hill at 50+ mph, I split off from my cycling club buddies and found myself stood next to a railway line. All I could think was, "I want more, I want to go faster!" A train whooshed past. My thoughts turned to, "What if I had stood in front of that train?" quickly countered by, "Well, I wasn't! So, something had to change." – I realised that something was missing in my life and I had to act.

After talking things through with my life coach, Michael Serwa, we realised that I wasn't passionate about building websites or designing logos, I had created a "job" for myself. However, I loved working with people, teaching them, creating products for them, building assets, and creating systems so they could charge more.

Michael said to me during one session, "Robin, it sounds to me like you're coaching!"

I spent three months rebranding and relaunched myself as a business coach. I had set a goal. I wanted to get ten clients within my first year. I created 14 clients in 6 weeks. At the age of 35 I am now running a 6-figure coaching business with great clients, and it is thanks to Michael, my coach, for kicking me into action and giving me the belief that I could do it.

Now, I coach other businesses owners and managers to do what I did. My niche is professional service businesses. From creative agencies turning over £20k+ per year to large accountancy firms turning over £2m+. I have created a number of my coaching tools to facilitate my fortnightly or monthly meetings with my clients.

I get a tremendous sense of achievement when I see my clients' businesses prosper and I have a goal to help 10,000 business owners in the next five years to double their turnover within six months using my tools. I can't do this all on a one-to-one basis, so I have created a number of coaching tools and programmes, and deliver regular talks and workshops to enable me to achieve my goal.

http://robinwaite.com

FEARLESS BUSINESS

Fearless Business is for anyone who is serious about growing their business, and potentially doubling your turnover and profit within the next 6 months.

But...you will become part of a family where I am the mother hen - I am incredibly proud of my brood whenever they have amazing wins, and lightbulb moments!!!

There are a number of things you will get access to:

- Weekly 2 Hour Webinar Panel Q&A
- Access to Discounted Breakthrough Sessions
- The Fearless Business Course (worth £195)
- The 7-Day Fearless Challenges (worth £95 each) once per month
- Accountability in the Fearless Business Group
- Message me anytime you like (don't take the p*ss) with you challenges and I'll jump on it ASAP.
- Online Business Startup Course (worth £30)
- Copies of Online Business Startup and pre-release copies of my next two books, before anyone else.

- Access to my little black book of contacts

You can apply to join at any time.

Fearless Business is ONLY £47/mth. And by application ONLY:

<u>http://fearless.biz</u>

That's priority access to me for only £47/mth which is an absolute bargain IMHO.

Interested??? Get online and apply.

READING LIST

Title	What It's About
Think and Grow Rich Napoleon Hill	We can learn to think like the rich we can discover wealth and success.
Built to Sell John Warrilow	Creating a Business That Can Thrive Without You
Go For No Richard Fenton and Andrea Waltz	Yes is the Destination, No is How You Get There
The Startup Coach Carl Reader	Other books help you talk the talk; the Teach Yourself Coach books will help you walk the walk.
The Lean Startup Eric Reis	How Today's Entrepreneurs Use Continuous Innovation to Create Radically Successful Businesses
The Prosperous Coach Steve Chandler and Rich Litvin	Increase Income and Impact for You and Your Clients
How to Be F*cking Awesome Dan Meredith	A kick up the backside to finally launch that business, start a new project you've been putting off or just become all round awesome.
24 Assets Daniel Priestley	Create a digital, scalable, valuable and fun business that will thrive in a fast changing world
The Phoenix Project Gene Kim and Kevin Behr	A Novel About IT, DevOps, and Helping Your Business Win
Principled Selling David Tovey	How to Win More Business Without Selling Your Soul
Elon Musk Ashlee Vance	How the Billionaire CEO of SpaceX and Tesla is Shaping our Future
From Good to Amazing Michael Serwa	No Bullshit Tips for The Life You Always Wanted

Title	What It's About
The Goal Jeff Cox, Eliyahu Goldratt	A Process of Ongoing Improvement
The Big Leap Gay Hedricks	Conquer Your Hidden Fear and Take Life to the Next Level
Sell or Be Sold Grant Cardone	How to Get Your Way in Business and Life
Flash Boys Michael Lewis	If you thought Wall Street was about alpha males standing in trading pits hollering at each other, think again
Life Leverage Rob Moore	How to Get More Done in Less Time, Outsource Everything & Create Your Ideal Mobile Lifestyle
Online Business Startup Robin Waite	The entrepreneur's guide to launching a fast, lean and profitable online venture
Outliers Malcolm Gladwell	The Story of Success

Printed in Great Britain
by Amazon